Pennsylvania

By Ann Heinrichs

Subject Consultant
Kathy Hale
Library Development Adviser
State Library of Pennsylvania, Harrisburg, Pennsylvania

Reading Consultant
Cecilia Minden-Cupp, PhD
Former Director of the Language and Literacy Program
Harvard Graduate School of Education
Cambridge, Massachusetts

Children's Press®
A Division of Scholastic Inc.
New York   Toronto   London   Auckland   Sydney
Mexico City   New Delhi   Hong Kong
Danbury, Connecticut

Designer: Herman Adler Design
Photo Researcher: Caroline Anderson
The photo on the cover shows a farm in Pennsylvania's Lehigh Valley.

Library of Congress Cataloging-in-Publication Data

Heinrichs, Ann.
  Pennsylvania / by Ann Heinrichs.
      p. cm. — (Rookie read-about geography)
  ISBN 0-516-24967-3 (lib. bdg.)   0-516-26719-1 (pbk.)
  1. Pennsylvania—Juvenile literature. 2. Pennsylvania—Geography—
Juvenile literature. I. Title. II. Series.
  F149.3.H455 2006
  974.8—dc22   2005018371

CHILDREN'S PRESS, and ROOKIE READ-ABOUT®,
and associated logos are trademarks and/or registered trademarks
of Scholastic Library Publishing. SCHOLASTIC and associated logos
are trademarks and/or registered trademarks of Scholastic Inc.

1 2 3 4 5 6 7 8 9 10 R 15 14 13 12 11 10 09 08 07 06

Which state is called the Keystone State?

Independence Day fireworks over the Philadelphia Museum of Art

It's Pennsylvania!

A keystone is a stone
used to build an arch.
Keystones hold other
stones in place. Early on,
many states depended
on Pennsylvania.

Pennsylvania is in the eastern part of the United States. Can you find Pennsylvania on this map?

The Allegheny Mountains

Mountains cover most of
Pennsylvania.

They include the Allegheny, Blue Ridge, and Pocono mountains.

The Pocono Mountains

Southeastern Pennsylvania has rich farmland. Corn, hay, and mushrooms are some of Pennsylvania's crops.

A Pennsylvania hay farm

Many farmers raise dairy cows for their milk. Milk is the state drink.

The Delaware River forms Pennsylvania's eastern edge. People enjoy boating, hiking, and camping along the river.

Northeastern Pennsylvania touches Lake Erie. This lake is one of the five Great Lakes. The Great Lakes are all connected to one another.

13

Forests cover more than half of Pennsylvania. Some of the forest trees are pine, hemlock, maple, and oak.

A Pennsylvania hemlock

Pennsylvania's state tree is the hemlock.

Many animals live in
Pennsylvania's forests.
The white-tailed deer is
the state animal.

The ruffed grouse is the
state bird.

Pennsylvania has cold, snowy winters. People there like to ski and sled.

Summers are warm.
Then people enjoy hiking
and boating.

Coal mining is important in Pennsylvania. Eastern Pennsylvania produces a lot of coal.

Miners dig the coal out of the ground. People burn coal to help make electricity.

Pennsylvania coal miners at work underground

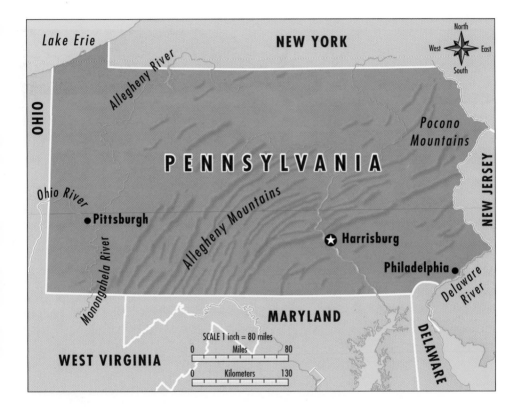

Lake Erie

NEW YORK

North
West ✦ East
South

OHIO

Allegheny River

Pocono
Mountains

PENNSYLVANIA

NEW JERSEY

Ohio River

Allegheny Mountains

●Pittsburgh

⭐ Harrisburg

Monongahela River

Philadelphia ●

Delaware
River

MARYLAND

SCALE 1 inch = 80 miles

0   Miles   80

0   Kilometers   130

WEST VIRGINIA

DELAWARE

Harrisburg is Pennsylvania's capital. Pennsylvania is the 32nd-largest state in the United States.

Philadelphia is the largest city in Pennsylvania. It has many historic buildings.

One of them is Independence Hall. The Declaration of Independence was signed there in 1776. That marked the beginning of the United States!

Independence Hall

The Ohio, Allegheny, and Monongahela rivers join in
Pittsburgh.

Pittsburgh is another
big city in Pennsylvania.
Three rivers flow together
there. They are the
Ohio, Allegheny, and
Monongahela rivers.

Would you like to visit
Pennsylvania someday?

What would you like to
do there?

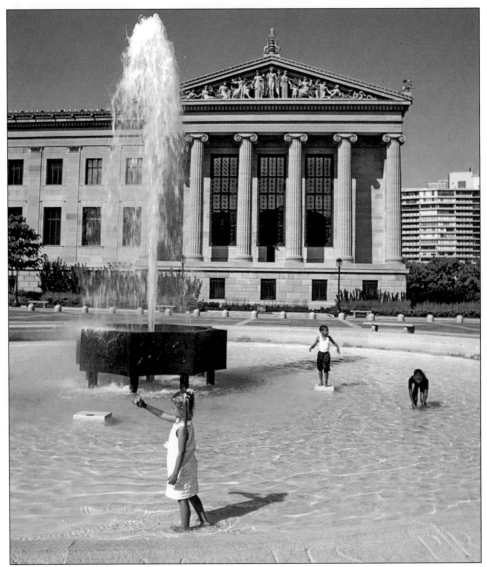
Young visitors splash in a Philadelphia fountain.

Words You Know

Allegheny Mountains

Delaware River

hemlock

Independence Hall

Lake Erie

white-tailed deer

Index

About the Author

Ann Heinrichs has written more than two hundred books for children.
She enjoys traveling to faraway countries. She lives in Chicago, Illinois.

Photo Credits

Photographs © 2006: AP/Wide World Photos: 18 (Dave Scherbenco/The
Citizens Voice), 26 (Keith Srakocic); Corbis Images: 3, 7, 13, 31 bottom left
(Bob Krist), 9 (Joe McDonald), 6, 30 top left (David Muench); Dembinsky
Photo Assoc.: 29 (Mark E. Gibson), 17 (Rod Planck); Getty Images: 8 (Ross M.
Horowitz/The Image Bank), 21 (Spencer Platt); Photo Researchers, NY: 15,
30 bottom (Michael P. Gadomski), 16, 31 bottom right (Stephen J. Krasemann);
PhotoEdit/Jeff Greenberg: 10, 30 top right; Robertstock.com/David Doody/
Camerique Inc.: 25, 31 top; Superstock, Inc.: cover (Michael P. Gadomski), 14;
The Image Works/Christopher Fitzgerald: 19.

Maps by Bob Italiano